D0574361

THE LIFE CYCLE OF AN

EARTHWORM

By L.L. Owens

Published by The Child's World®
1980 Lookout Drive
Mankato, MN 56003-1705
800-599-READ
www.childsworld.com

The Child's World®: Mary Berendes, Publishing Director
The Design Lab: Kathleen Petelinsek, design
Red Line Editorial: Editorial direction

Photographs ©: Alasdair Thomson/iStockphoto, cover (top right, bottom left), 1 (top right, bottom left), 3; Oxford Scientific/Photolibrary, cover (top left, bottom right), 1 (top left, bottom right), 29, 30; iStockphoto, 5, 10, 13, 18, 21; David Anderson/Shutterstock Images, 6; Science Photo Library/Photolibrary, 9; Peter Arnold Images/Photolibrary, 14, 31 (bottom); Shutterstock Images, 17, 31 (top); Fotolia, 22, 25; Melinda Fawver/Shutterstock Images, 26

4822 7002   03/12

ISBN: 978-1-60973-148-9
LCCN: 2011927736

Printed in the United States of America
Mankato, MN
July 2011
PA02089

CONTENTS

Life Cycles...4

Earthworms...7

Hatching...15

New Earthworms...16

Finding Food...19

Earthworm Eggs...24

Life Cycle Diagram...30

Web Sites and Books...32

Glossary...32

Index...32

LIFE CYCLES

Every living thing has a life cycle. A life cycle is the steps a living thing goes through as it grows and changes. Humans have a life cycle. Animals have a life cycle. Plants have a life cycle, too.

A cycle is something that happens over and over again. A life cycle begins with the start of a new life. It continues as a plant or creature grows. And it keeps going as one living thing creates another, or **reproduces**—and the cycle starts over again.

An earthworm's life cycle has three main steps: egg, juvenile, and adult earthworm.

Like humans, earthworms have life cycles, too.

An earthworm's body is made of many segments.

EARTHWORMS

The earthworm belongs to a group of animals called **annelids**. Annelids are animals with no backbones. They have soft, flexible bodies. An earthworm has a long body that can wiggle, twist, and curl. Its body is divided into many rings, called segments, and each segment is almost exactly like the others.

One segment on each end is different. At the back end is a tail. At the front is a tiny head and a simple brain. An earthworm has a mouth but no teeth or eyes. Sensitive skin on its body helps it detect light. An earthworm breathes by taking in air through its slimy skin.

Each body segment has four pairs of tiny bristles. The stiff bristles help an earthworm move without legs. The bristles are very strong. The worm can move its bristles in and out of its skin. The bristles grab hold of the soil and help a worm crawl and tunnel into the ground.

Stiff bristles on an earthworm's body help it crawl across and dig into the soil.

Earthworms come in unexpected colors. This is a red worm.

More than 4,000 kinds of earthworms exist on Earth. They live just about everywhere you can find moist, unfrozen soil. Earthworms often found in North America include night crawlers, red worms, and field worms. Most earthworms are between a few inches (7 or 8 cm) and 3 feet (1 m) long. The smallest earthworm is shorter than your thumb. But the Giant South African earthworm is much larger. It can grow up to 22 feet (7 m) long.

Earthworms need to live in damp places. Their skin must stay moist in order to breathe. If an earthworm gets lost on a hot sidewalk for too long, its skin will dry out. The worm will stop breathing and die.

To keep moist, earthworms stay underground during the day. They dig long burrows, or tunnels, in the soil. They can also be found under rocks, in piles of damp leaves, or under fallen trees. They might come out when the sun goes down.

Earthworms may come above ground when it rains if their burrows get too wet. On a cloudy, damp day or at night, they can search for food in the grass without drying out.

When it rains, earthworms may come above ground.

Baby earthworms are clear when they first hatch, but quickly get darker.

HATCHING

Baby earthworms hatch from eggs inside **cocoons**. An earthworm cocoon may be the size of a rice grain or a chicken egg, depending on the size of the earthworm parent. Usually a few baby earthworms grow inside a cocoon, feeding on its nutrients. When the babies grow too big, they hatch from the cocoon as tiny see-through earthworms.

NEW EARTHWORMS

Juveniles, or young earthworms, look almost like adult earthworms but are much smaller and paler. The color of their bodies begins darkening from the day they leave their cocoon. Most earthworms are brown, gray, pink, or red. Often their body color matches the soil where they live.

No parent helps the baby after it hatches, but the baby needs food right away. Baby earthworms feed on their cocoons. Then they wriggle off to find food on top of and in the soil. Baby earthworms know how to dig from the moment they hatch. A night crawler may dig a burrow 6 feet (2 m) deep.

Earthworm bodies darken as they grow.

Worm waste, called castings, keep soil rich with nutrients.

FINDING FOOD

Without teeth, earthworms must suck food into their mouths. They swallow tiny bits of soil, dead leaves, and rotting insects. They also swallow tiny rocks. The rocks help grind up food inside worms' bodies. Then worms can absorb the nutrients their bodies need. What they cannot use is pushed out the back end of worms as waste, called castings.

Castings still have plenty of nutrients that plants can use to grow. Earthworms are known as **decomposers**. Their eating habits help break down dead and rotting plants and animals and recycle them into the soil.

Earthworms usually search for their food at night when it is cooler. Some **predators** eat earthworms at night when they are above ground. These predators include raccoons, skunks, and spiders. Birds hunt worms during the day. And moles and underground animals hunt worms day or night.

When earthworms are born, they have senses that help them survive. Their skin detects smell, light, feel, and taste. Their senses tell them when to hide from other animals, where to find food, and what the weather is like.

A hungry mole eats an earthworm.

When an earthworm becomes an adult, it grows a thick band, called a saddle, near its head.

As earthworms grow, they must stay away from predators and find the food they need. Earthworms smell and taste moldy leaves or other parts of their surroundings. They also feel vibrations. If a hungry mole digs nearby, the worms feel the movement and crawl away.

About three months to one year after hatching, an earthworm is fully grown. An adult earthworm has a thick band near its head. The band, sometimes called a saddle, is needed for the next step in the life cycle. The earthworm is ready to reproduce, or create new earthworms.

EARTHWORM EGGS

Unlike dogs, birds, or people, each earthworm has both male and female reproductive parts. The female parts make eggs, and the male parts make sperm. When it is time to mate, two earthworms find a safe place and line up their bodies. They trade sperm to **fertilize** each other's eggs. Then each worm crawls off alone.

The saddle band creates a tube of slime that holds the fertilized eggs. The worm crawls out of the tube and it closes, making a cocoon for the eggs. Then the worm leaves the cocoon in a safe place in the soil.

Earthworms mate by lining up their bodies.

Adult earthworms do not raise their young.

Reproduction is the only role of earthworm parents. They may reproduce several times during their lives, though. It is hard to tell how long earthworms have lived. Adults look the same as they get older. On average, earthworms live about two years. But many are eaten before becoming adults.

The unhatched baby earthworms grow inside the cocoon for two or more weeks. During the winter, they will stay in the cocoon for months. The unhatched young get the nutrients they need from inside their cocoons. At last, tiny earthworms wiggle out. They are ready to crawl off on their own. The life cycle of the earthworm continues.

Each earthworm cocoon has a few eggs inside.

LIFE CYCLE DIAGRAM

Eggs in Cocoon

Adult Earthworm

Juvenile

Web Sites

Visit our Web site for links about the life cycle of an earthworm: **childsworld.com/links**

Note to Parents, Teachers, and Librarians: We routinely verify our Web links to make sure they are safe and active sites. So encourage your readers to check them out!

Books

Blaxland, Beth. *Earthworms, Leeches, and Sea Worms.* New York: Chelsea House, 2002.

French, Vivian. *Yucky Worms.* Somerville, MA: Candlewick Press, 2009.

Lunis, Natalie. *Wiggly Earthworms.* New York: Bearport Publishing, 2009.

Glossary

annelids (AN-nuh-lidz): Annelids are animals that do not have backbones and have soft, flexible bodies with bristles to move. Earthworms are annelids.

cocoons (kuh-KOONS): Earthworm cocoons are protective cases for earthworm eggs. Earthworm babies grow in cocoons.

decomposers (dee-kum-POZE-urz): Decomposers are living things that break down dead plants and animals. Earthworms are decomposers.

fertilize (FUR-tuh-lize): To fertilize is when a male reproductive cell joins a female reproductive cell to create a new life. Earthworms fertilize each other's eggs.

predators (PRED-uh-turs): Predators are animals that hunt and eat other animals. Moles are predators of earthworms.

reproduces (ree-pruh-DOOS-ez): If an animal or plant reproduces, it produces offspring. An earthworm reproduces to make new earthworms.

Index

adult, 4, 23, 27
annelid, 7

body, 7–8, 16, 19
bristles, 8

castings, 19
cocoon, 15–16, 24, 28
color, 15–16

decomposer, 19
digging, 12, 16

eating, 15–16, 19–20
egg, 4, 15, 24

field worm, 11

Giant South African earthworm, 11
growth, 11, 23

habitat, 11–12
hatching, 15, 28

juvenile, 4, 16

life span, 27

night crawler, 11, 16

predators, 20, 23

rain, 12
red worm, 11
reproduce, 4, 23, 24, 27
reproductive parts, 24

saddle, 23–24
segment, 7, 8
senses, 20, 23
size, 11